The Winter Road

BOOKS BY LOUIS JENKINS

Just Above Water (1997)

Nice Fish: New and Selected Prose Poems (1995)

All Tangled Up With the Living (1991)

An Almost Human Gesture (1987)

The Winter Road

Prose Poems
by

Louis Jenkins

HOLY COW! PRESS · DULUTH, MINNESOTA · 2000

Grateful acknowledgement is made to the editors and publishers
of the following magazines in which some of these poems first appeared:
*Agni, Great River Review, Key Satch(el), Lake Country Journal, Luna, Manhattan
Review, Midwest Quarterly, North Life, Potato Eyes, Puerto del Sol, Seneca Review,
Snowy Egret, Solo Flyer, Willow Springs.*

Several of these poems were originally published as part of *The Third Image:
Words and Pictures*, a collaborative work with Richard C. Johnson.

Thanks to Patricia Canelake, Stephen Dahl, Jean Jacobson,
Rick Johnson, and Jim Perlman.

Special thanks to Robert Bly who has helped so often in so many ways.

Library of Congress Cataloging-in-Publication Data
Jenkins, Louis, 1942-
The winter road : poems / Louis Jenkins
p. cm.
ISBN 0-930100-14-X
1. Memory—Poetry. 2. Prose poems, American. I. Title.
PS3560.E488 W5 2000   00-061360
811'.54—dc21

Holy Cow! Press books are distributed to the trade by Consortium Book Sales &
Distribution, 1045 Westgate Drive, Saint Paul, Minnesota 55114. Our books are
available through all major library distributors and jobbers, and through most small
press distributors, including Bookpeople and Small Press Distribution.
For personal orders, catalogs, or other information, please write to:

Holy Cow! Press
Post Office Box 3170
Mount Royal Station
Duluth, Minnesota 55803

CONTENTS

THREE

FOUR

For Ann and Lars
and for all my family

ONE

STORY

The things that happen willy-nilly in life, lawsuit, gum disease, romance... must be given, if not meaning, at least some context. Each has to be incorporated immediately into the story you tell yourself. And the sooner the better. In order to avoid unpleasant surprises, things should be written in before they occur. But now I've gotten ahead of myself, my shadow stretching out thirty feet ahead on the winter road: enormous feet, wide legs, big fat ass and a torso tapering away to a tiny, pin head. This is not a true likeness, of course, the distortion caused by my distance from the sun. But it gives you the idea. The truth, the absolute truth, is like absolute zero, more a hypothesis than an actuality. If you could experience it you wouldn't like it. It's cold enough as it is. The truth is an imaginary point, like the vanishing point. It's as if there were a point to this story. As if when you got to the end you could remember what happened in the beginning.

THE TELEPHONE

In the old days, telephones were made of whale vertebrae and were big and heavy enough to fight off an intruder. The telephone had a special place in the front hallway, a shrine, a kind of grotto built into the wall and when the phone rang it was serious business. "Hello." "One if by land and two if by sea." "What?" "Unto you a child is born." "What?" "What did he say?" "Something about the Chalmers' barn." The voice was carried by a single strand of bare wire running from coast to coast, wrapped around a Coke bottle stuck on a tree branch, dipping low over the swamp, it was the party line, all your neighbors in a row, out one ear and in another. "We have a bad connection, I'm having trouble understanding you."

Nowadays telephones are made of recycled plastic bags and have multiplied to the point where they have become a major nuisance. The phone might ring at you from anywhere; the car, the bathroom, under the couch cushion. Everyone hates the telephone. No one uses the telephone anymore so telephones, out of habit or boredom or loneliness perhaps, call one another. "Please leave a message at the tone." "I'm sorry, this is a courtesy call. We'll call back at a more convenient time. There is no message."

TUMBLING TUMBLEWEEDS

Out on the great plains, where I was born, the wind blows constantly. When I was a kid I'd get 35 cents and run as hard as I could to the Lotta-Burger or the movie theater only to find it had blown away. Going home was no better. Sometimes it would take a couple of days to find my house. Under these conditions it was impossible to get acquainted with the neighbors. It was a shock to open the front door and be faced with the county jail, the Pentecostal Church or Aunt Erma carrying two large suitcases. Trash from all over the state caught and piled up at the edge of town and during the windiest times of spring sometimes whole days blew away in a cloud of dust. I feel my natural lifespan may have been shortened by the experience. Still, it was a great place to grow up. As the old boy said, "You can have those big cities, people all jammed together. Give me some wide-open spaces." In the morning out on the plains you have a couple of cups of coffee, get all wound up and go like hell across an open field, try to bounce, clear both ditches and the highway so you don't get caught in the barbed wire, fly from one fenced-in nothing to another, hit the ground and keep on rolling.

CORONADO

Coronado came up from Mexico in search of the life of the imagination. The Zunis said "Oh God, here comes Coronado and those Spaniards." The Zunis drew a line on the ground with cornmeal and said "OK Coronado cross that line and you'll be sorry." But of course he crossed. The Zunis said, "Seven Cities of Gold? Go see the Pueblos." So on he went, but the great cities did not appear, only mud houses. The Pueblos said "Oh yeah, Seven Cities of Gold, they're over northeast, way over, maybe five hundred or a thousand miles." So he set out again. There was nothing, day after day, no gold, no silver, not even an ATM, just the wind blowing through the prairie grass. Coronado was a determined man who knew that hard work and patience would be rewarded. But when he got to Kansas he realized that this had to be a joke or else that someone had been badly misinformed.

MUDHOLE

Life has no meaning. Right at the center of anything you can name there's a big nothing, an emptiness large enough to drive a truck through. But nobody dies just because of that. My grandfather farmed for years around a mudhole right in the middle of his already meager acreage. A kind of curving ditch known as "the creek" though it seldom held any water. The mark of the harrow and the mark of the plow followed the contour of the bank making a pleasing pattern in the dirt. The way the lines of a poem are pleasing (something about seagulls, the sun going down and the column of dust rising behind the tractor, visible even from the County Line Bar two miles away) or bars of music, which has no meaning either. Someone can take a perfectly good drinking song, turn it into an anthem, people enlist, and things get a whole lot worse. But meanwhile, back at the tavern, the music goes on and so does the drinking.

SUNFLOWERS

The few we managed to twist off their tough, sap-sticky stalks Mother would not allow inside. So we put them in an empty fruit jar on the back porch where they slumped over forgotten and died. They grew everywhere, in the ditches, around the barns, the bright yellow and brown whizzing past you in the car on the Saturday drive into town like spots before your eyes. What fun! Sprawling into the untended fields, over the abandoned farms, jumping up and down in the back until the seat springs broke.

A MIRACLE

When my father was eight he cut his foot on something in the high grass and got blood poisoning. Inexorably the red line rose toward the heart and the doctors could do nothing. Then one evening just at dark the gypsy healer came to the door. No one had called her, an old woman with many layers of odd clothes, long skirts and a man's raincoat. She examined the foot, muttered some words, a prayer perhaps, and said "Here. The poison is here." She made a swift cut with a small knife that seemed to appear from nowhere. "You must soak the foot in very hot water and Epsom salts for one hour, three times a day. In three days the child will be well." And it worked. Strangely, the healer would take no pay. She went back to the gypsy camp, to the horses and wagons, the dark-skinned men in white shirts, the ragged children. One morning, a week later, my grandfather woke to find that all the chickens were gone, every single one, only some feathers on the floor of the silent coop. The gypsies were gone too, vanished in the night. Miracles always have a cost. When one thing is repaired another breaks. When something is healed, something else dies. So the old woman took nothing, knowing God would provide.

THE PREACHER

When times were hard, no work on the railroad, no work down on the farm, some of my ancestors took to preaching. It was not so much what was said as the way in which it was said. "The horn shall sound and the dog will bark and though you be on the highest mountain or down in the deepest valley when the darkness comes then you will lie down, and as the day follows the night you will surely rise again. The Lord our God hath made both heaven and earth. Oh, my dear brothers and sisters we know so well the ways of this world, think then what heaven must be like." It required a certain presence, a certain authority. The preacher was treated with respect and kept at a bit of a distance, like a rattler. There wasn't much money in it but it was good for maybe a dozen eggs or a chicken dinner now and then.

A HILL OF BEANS

As children we were given inaccurate information. Things turned out to be much different than we were led to believe. Adults were not entirely to blame for this because most of them had no more idea what was going on than we did and found themselves bewildered at every turn, baffled by the impossible complexities of life. So instead of real insight we were given homilies and aphorisms. "Life is no bed of roses." "You can lead a horse to water but you can't make him drink." Of course society has changed radically, even in my lifetime. Therefore the rather agrarian quality of these sayings has caused them to lose some of their original impact. "You aren't going to amount to a hill of beans." Which, to me, suggested laziness, shiftlessness, failure, poverty, rambling discourse, idle speculation.... I suspect that "a hill of beans" refers to the fact that beans are of little value even in large quantities and also that they make very poor hills. Yet, I can't help imagining a really important hill, a great Bunker Hill of beans, or a San Juan Hill of slippery pork and beans up which a frustrated Teddy Roosevelt is trying to charge.

CRIPPLE CREEK

Five of us crammed into my car. I drove. I think it was my idea. I'd read something and I had a map. For some reason I thought I knew what I was doing. And nobody objected! It seems amazing to me now, how willing they were to risk their lives, careening around the mountain backroads. I think we made it. We survived. Where were we going? Was there someone I was longing to see? I don't remember. It was important. But no matter how much I think about it, there is no destination. Just the little green car flying around the switchbacks, rocks, pines, the clear sky, the wheels throwing gravel into the air and over the edge.

HIGH FINANCE

"It takes money to make money," my father said, "you have to have something to invest." We all nodded and made affirmative, muttering sounds. "Take care of the nickels and the dollars will take care of themselves," my mother said. "Some people are born with a talent for making money," my father said, "but you've got to have a start, a little bit of luck," "Thrift. Thrift and hard work," Mother said. We all stared silently into our coffee cups. "Owning your own business," Father said, as if he hadn't heard Mother at all, "that's the way to make money. You'll never make any money working for someone else." "Nonsense," Mother said, "that's all pie in the sky." "Pie in the sky," we thought, "mmm . . . pie in the sky!" Pie with great cumulus mounds of ice cream, served on silver platters, inside those castles in the air. Pie in the sky . . . cloudberry pie.

CIMARRON

"Cimarron roll on
 to my lonely song."
 Sons of the Pioneers

Except for periodic floods the river didn't so much roll as kind
of amble. "A mile wide and a foot deep," they said. In dry times
the sandy riverbottom was like a beach, a shore with no ocean.
But the water was moving, leaving behind the bloated carcass of
a hog rotting in the sun, carp and catfish trapped in rapidly
evaporating pools, a whole steam engine sunk beneath the
quicksand, a house collapsed where the bank eroded away. The
river wandered away as in a dream, no explanations, no parting
words, the door ajar, newspapers blown across the floor, dirty
dishes left in the sink. . . .

RADIO

When I was a kid I listened to the radio late at night. I tuned it low as I could and put my ear right up next to it because my dad didn't like it. He'd say, "Turn off that radio. It's after midnight!" No matter how low I tuned it he could still hear, from down the hall and through two closed doors. He was tired. It had been a long day and this was just one more thing, the final thing, keeping him from the sleep, the absolute dead silence he wanted. As for me, whatever music I was listening to, some rock station way down on the border, probably, "100,000 watts of pure power," has become even more faint over the years. But I can still hear it.

TWO

WIND IN THE TREES

You could live on the go like the wind with what seems like a purpose or at least a direction, but no home, reckless, pushy, with an attention deficit disorder, no more than a name, really. People will say "That guy, you know. . . ." But if you stand still long enough you will be given an identity. You could live like the trees, parochial, rooted and restless, prone to hysteria. You could write letters to the editor. Living in the woods you get a lot of ideas about what God is up to. You'd have a family, parents, grandparents, aunts and uncles all close around you until, if you are lucky, they recede, one by one, into the peripheral haze of memory. Finally, some space, a clearing, a place to fall.

PILGRIMAGES

People come from hundreds of miles away to walk along this shore. They like it especially when the sea is violent and flings itself against the rocks. The solitary pilgrim walks head down, hands in pockets, collar turned up against the wind, muttering "I know what you mean, I know just what you mean." Then he goes away. As he must, as we all must. Even if you sleep every night at the door of the temple, in shadow of the shrine and sell maps of the Holy City, the time will come to go on pilgrimage. Suppose for thirty years you've been holding a downspout to a stone wall. It's not a job you intended to keep for so long, but time slips away. Then one day you're offered a new position, suspending a muffler and tailpipe, trying to maintain the integrity of a Chrysler product. How can you refuse? Somewhere the restless heart must be satisfied. So away you go, in a cloud of smoke, and the long, winding road turns out to be short. And straight as a dog's throat.

YOUR SHIP

Officials of the Kalends Ship Line today denied having any knowledge, "at this time," of the *Danaïd* or its cargo and were unavailable for further comment. Nevertheless your ship is out there somewhere, sailing under a flag of convenience, bound for either Marseilles or Jakarta, rolling on the oily swells, the cargo shifting slightly with each rise and fall.

Last night during middle watch the mate caught sight of a woman below decks. He recognized her immediately as the woman he'd seen in the hotel lounge the night before they sailed. Long hair and heels, the jacket of her suit slung over her shoulder, she was whistling a little tune as she turned and disappeared down a dimly lighted passageway.

APPARITION

She said "Take me to California, I want to see the ocean." As soon as I said yes I knew it was trouble. Right away I could see myself on the streets of Los Angeles without my wallet or maybe even without my pants. As it turned out I got no farther than Utah before I found myself hallooing into culvert openings. Now I've got myself into this and can't see a graceful way out. . . . The next morning bright as a penny, another sunny honeymoon on the dusty road, all on my own with the grasshoppers and the rattlesnakes, still a hundred miles from anywhere. She was beautiful and said all the silly things I wanted to hear. She said "Come with me and you can have your own life."

JAZZ POEM

I always wanted to write one of those Jazz poems. You know the kind, where it's three a.m. in some incredibly smoky, out of the way, little club in Chicago or New York, April 14, 1954 (it's always good to give the date) and there are only a few sleepy people left in the place, vacant tables with half-empty glasses, overturned chairs . . . and then Bird or LeRoy or someone plays this incredible solo and it's like, it's like . . . well, you just should have been there. . . . The poet was there and you understand from the poem that jazz is hip, intellectual, cool but also earthy and soulful, as the poet must be as well because he really digs this stuff. Unfortunately, I grew up listening to rock and roll and decidedly unhip country music and it just doesn't work to say you should have been in Gary Hofstadter's rec room July 24, 1961, sipping a Pepsi, listening to Duane Eddy on 45's.

BAD PLACE

The story is that the Dacotah would never make their camp here, that the horses would bolt whenever they came near. It's a bad place and nothing can be done about it. No amount of urban renewal will help. The brick crumbles and the boards rot. There is broken glass under the street light and nightshade grows in the alley. It's a low place where the air is bad, a kind of depression located halfway up and halfway down. This place is the very center of a Bermuda triangle that's bounded by Thanksgiving, Christmas and New Year's. Uncle Karl is drunk and Aunt Liz is crying. . . . This is the place that, everyday, no matter which route you take, you have to walk through on your way home.

MAY

Finally, no amount
of kindness or
generosity will help.
In May the song sparrow
returns. Hidden
in the spring green
his only gift is his song,
all the sweeter because
it isn't meant for you.

THE PROSE POEM

The prose poem is not a real poem, of course. One of the major differences is that the prose poet is simply too lazy or too stupid to break the poem into lines. But all writing, even the prose poem, involves a certain amount of skill, just the way throwing a wad of paper, say, into a wastebasket at a distance of twenty feet, requires a certain skill, a skill that, though it may improve hand-eye coordination, does not lead necessarily to an ability to play basketball. Still, it takes practice and thus gives one a way to pass the time, chucking one paper after another at the basket, while the teacher drones on about the poetry of Tennyson.

AS THE LIGHT TURNS GREEN

The faith of saints is absolute. There is order beyond all this dying, eating and begetting. Beyond the work week there is reason that, in the fullness of time, will be made manifest. A saint is lifted as a solitary star into the firmament. One by one, as the light turns green, we mortals merge into the Great Flow but a saint will cross six lanes of traffic to reach the posited exit.

FLORIDA

This morning at the university I passed a young woman in the hall who was wearing an orange t-shirt with FLORIDA printed on the front in large white letters. Naturally I thought of citrus fruit. I thought of orange groves with workers tending the smudge pots on cold nights. I thought of Wallace Stevens in his white suit, walking barefoot on the beach, carrying his shoes with the socks tucked inside, and I imagined the moon over Miami. I have never been to Florida but I know there are drug dealers, red tide, walking catfish, Republicans, Disney World . . . . Still, the citrus fruit is very good this time of year and when I peel an orange and look out the window at the snow and the rough spruce trees turning black in the early dusk it seems like a miracle. One taste and I know there is a world beyond my imagining. It's impossible, like love, yet it really exists.

AQUI

People say things you can't understand, the air is strange and the pale, daytime moon is in the wrong position. So far from home all that you assumed becomes stretched to a thread, more narrow than the highway through the Sierra de Guanajuato, stretched so thin, in fact, that for fear that it might break, one is careful, while lying in the shade of the bougainvillea, not to make any sudden moves. Now, in the Plaza de Nuestra Senora De La Luz, in the midafternoon heat, almost nothing moves. The burro, loaded, as ever, with fifty-kilo sacks, is tied to the Jacaranda tree, where he has always been, where he always will be. He twitches an ear when a fly lands on it—but not when the bells of the Oratorio begin their clamor.

CEREMONY

One day you cross an invisible line and everything is changed. But what? It is as if you had crossed the international dateline, all at once it's another day. Now, everything you looked forward to is suddenly behind. What did you hope for anyway? And why? Neither love nor money will help. Your previous life is hearsay and is inadmissible as evidence. Perhaps, during the night while you slept, there was a ceremony to mark the occasion, a party. Books and papers are scattered everywhere and, obviously, someone has stolen your reading glasses. Hijinks. Perhaps King Neptune himself, in his iron crown, presided over the court as you were ushered into a new world. It's morning. The ship sails on, same as ever, into the blue.

RIVER GORGE

I could carve out
a little place for myself
in 10,000 years or so,
but long before that life
would have gone all strange
and none of the landmarks
would be familiar.
Like the water
I'm just passing through,
only I'm not taking
anything with me.

PICNIC ON THE SHORE

Shore grass growing
among the big rocks
enduring year after year.
This is the way to live.
A simple life,
the proper arrangement
of a few elements.
But here you are
standing on slippery stone,
trying to balance
a full plate and a cup.
What with the wrappers,
the flies and the wind,
already things
have gotten out of hand.

THREE

DULUTH

"A baby, eh?" That's all he says. She never says he's the father and he never admits it but they get married anyway. This way the city gains another citizen. But for each one that's born another dies or moves away and things remain more or less the same. The mayor has been dead for several years but he does a better job that way so we keep him in office. We prefer it quiet, understated. At one o'clock Sunday morning the snow plow passes with its flashing blue light and then, ten minutes later, a car, silent, muffled by the snow. That's all. A light still shines in the attic apartment of a large house two blocks over. These old houses, once the mansions of mining millionaires and lumber barons, are full of secrets. Some properties have been completely restored and in others people keep bears as pets. If you are outside around dawn you might catch a glimpse of someone taking the bear for a walk and think "Why would anyone want a big dog like that? But then. . ." you say to yourself, "there are all these new people in town."

CHANGE

All those things that have gone from your life, moon boots, TV trays and the Soviet Union, that seem to have vanished, are really only changed, dinosaurs did not disappear from the earth but evolved into birds and crock pots became bread makers. Everything around you changes. It seems at times (only for a moment) that your wife, the woman you love, might actually be your first wife in another form. It's a thought not to be pursued . . . . Nothing is the same as it used to be. Except you, of course, you haven't changed . . . well, slowed down a bit, perhaps. It's more difficult nowadays to deal with the speed of change, disturbing to suddenly find yourself brushing your teeth with what appears to be a flashlight. But essentially you are the same as ever, constant in your instability.

IRON

Iron is purely masculine, containing perhaps too many Y chromosomes. Iron lacks the flexibility and strength of steel which is tempered by the feminine element. Iron lacks delicacy, but does not lack courage. Iron is hard work and sweat. Iron is passion without finesse. A long time ago a man discovered that he could make an impressive sound by dragging a large piece of iron through a field of stones. Iron is divorce, child-support payments, poorly-planned crime, dishes in the sink, wool socks drying over the coal stove. Out back there's the hulk of a '57 Chevy still awaiting restoration. What glowed red hot in youth is cold as a pump handle in middle age.

NORTHERN LIGHT

The light is everything. Matisse and Monet had plenty of light. They were profligate, slopping Mediterranean sun everywhere. Vermeer had to buy it, a little at a time, import it from Africa or someplace. It ruined him, finally, the costly gold leaf and the precious ultramarine. In the north the light has to be concentrated and focused. Each detail must be accounted for, placed carefully just this side of darkness. Here a bit of sun on a yellow building, here light from the window, illuminating her face and highlighting the folds of the letter in her hand. News from far away, we imagine. Difficult to say if it's good news or bad, but then, any word the light brings is better than no word at all.

FIRE DANGER

When conditions are right, it takes only the smallest spark to set the entire forest on fire. Like love, kindled by the merest glance or a smile, even though the two of you have nothing at all in common. It's the chance arrangement of positive and negative ions. You say, "We have so much in common, so much more than Elaine and I ever have." You say, "Sometimes we talk for hours. We have so much to talk about." All summer, all through September and October the winds stirred in the dry timber. Now in November, the leaves are down, and the cold rain falls day after day. "So what?" you say to yourself, "So what?" You tell your friends, "It's wonderful. I've never felt like this before. I'm so unhappy." And your friends run away when they see you coming.

LATE OCTOBER ABOVE LAKE SUPERIOR

A north wind shakes the last few yellow leaves clinging to a thin popple tree. It's easy to tell what's coming. Old leaves must fall to make way for the new. That's all well and good as long as it's not your turn to go. Keep the dead waiting! Keep the unborn waiting! There's not much to this life anyway, some notions, some longings that come and go like the sea, like sun and shadow played across the stone. This weather is not so bad if you can find a place among the rocks out of the wind.

HEAVEN

Heaven is a state of such perfection that it is difficult to describe. It lacks the irregularities of life that make a good story, that make people realize they are alive. But, of course, in heaven people aren't alive. There is little to say of the day-to-day as there are no days or nights. So conversations begin "Back when I was alive. . . ." or "When I lived in Chicago. . . ." In my dream we were riding in a car, we were in back. I fell asleep and dreamed that you touched my hair, while I slept. It was a dream within a dream, an infinity of mirrors, reflecting nothing, finally. When I woke from one or another of my dreams I found a hairpin in my hair that must have been one of yours. In heaven I will carry it in my pocket. That is, if in heaven we have pockets.

PIONEER FARM

Think of spending the winter alone here, in this two room cabin. Think of spending it here with someone else. The settlers were frugal. They used newspaper for toilet tissue, newspaper for chinking between the logs, the words carefully mouthed and puzzled over then shoved into a crack. Once a month someone made the long trip into town to sell the eggs and buy a newspaper. They used feed bags for dresses, harness leather for door hinges, snot for bubble gum. The Bible was their only book. Mother was crazy and Father was a tyrant. The eldest daughter ran off with a sewing machine salesman. The first son ran away and set up his own little monarchy, just like this one. Everyone is gone now, even the owl who used to roost in the barn. It's not a good place for a farm, the growing season too short, the ground too rocky. What I hate most is the lingering sanctimonious air, the condescending forgiveness.

MAILBOXES

Some are brightly painted and large as if anticipating great packages. Most are smaller, gray and dented with rust spots, some held together with rope or duct tape, having been slapped more than once by the snow plow. Still they seem hopeful . . . perhaps a Village Shopper or a credit card offer. . . . Once in while one raises a modest tin flag. "I have something. It isn't much. I'd like you to take it." All along Highway 16, on Hunter Road and Dahl Road, past Cane Lake, past the gravel pit, and the last refrigerator shot full of holes and dumped into the swamp, mailboxes reach out on extended arms, all the way to the end of the route where balsam and spruce crowd together in the ditches, reaching out. . . .

THE LOON

A loon surfaces suddenly not more than ten feet from the boat. How rare to be so close to this wild and beautiful bird! An unexpected joy. But quick as thought he vanishes, slips silently under water again. The loon is neither memory nor desire nor anything you imagined. If you are observant you will notice that the loon does not regard your sudden appearance as particularly beneficial. And when he surfaces again, far behind your back, he is not laughing, though it seems so.

SUNDAY MORNING

Sunday mornings in church when you were a child, then dinner at Aunt Pearl's house. The endless afternoon in the backyard with only her arthritic Pekinese for company, while inside the adults talked on and on about people who were dead. Think of learning the multiplication tables, true love, and the hours you spent sitting on the edge of the bed in your shorts biting your fingernails. You learned to smoke and to drive a car, how to cook spaghetti. Maybe all of that counts for something and someone somewhere has kept score. Something like Social Security. Maybe one day you will be compensated (with certain deductions and penalties, no doubt) for your accumulated life experience. Enough, perhaps, for a double-wide modular home on some rather low ground in an outlying district of what may not be heaven, but could certainly be a lot worse.

HOCKEY

Ice hockey makes very little sense to the innocent bystander. Yet people in this area are passionate about the sport, so, like religion and politics, it is a subject best not brought up in polite conversation. The players, in their heavily padded uniforms (which for some strange reason include shorts) and skates, all trying to whack the puck into one or the other of the nets, seems, to the uninitiated viewer, a very approximate operation, something like trying to knit while wearing boxing gloves. One of the biggest problems for the spectator and, evidently, for the players as well, is that the puck is hard to see. It is so small and shoots across the ice at great speed or gets caught beneath a mass of fallen players. This causes a great deal of frustration among the players, which they vent upon one another. Long ago, before we became so politically correct, hockey was played using a recently detached human head as a puck. More brutal perhaps, but it's much easier to follow the puck.

OUR NEW HOUSE

Our new house is too small to hold a real ghost or even a poltergeist. It is more a cottage than a house, nevertheless there are things that go bump in the night, enough to wake you from a sound sleep. We are not yet quite settled in and our possessions have not all decided on a place. One morning I found my toothbrush on top of the refrigerator and today apparently, the geranium prefers to suffer next to the window. Everything seems to desire change. A young woman marries, against her parent's wishes, a man from New Jersey of doubtful reputation. In subsequent generations the family knack for mathematics is lost, as is the talent for horsemanship. What remains is a characteristic willfulness and the prominent nose. Everything wants to move. Even the flour canister musters just enough sleepy energy to fall from the shelf to the floor, spilling its contents. Yet it maintains a slightly ridiculous attitude of dignity even in abject defeat.

ROCK COLLECTING

On Hegberg Road
I found a really big agate,
big as my fist.
I washed off the dirt
in the ditch water and
on closer examination
discovered that
it wasn't an agate after all,
just an ordinary reddish
colored rock.
What a relief!
I could drop the rock
back in the road.
I could go on
with my life.

FOUR

BACK HOME

The place I lived as a child, the sharecropper's farmhouse with its wind-bent mulberry trees and rusted farm machinery has completely vanished. Now there's nothing but plowed fields for miles in any direction. When I asked around in town no one remembered the family. No way to verify my story. In fact, there's no evidence that any of what I remember actually happened, or that the people I knew ever existed. There was my uncle Axel, for instance, who spent most of his life moving from one job to another, trying to "find himself." He should have saved himself the trouble. I moved away from there a long time ago, when I was a young man, and came to the cold spruce forests of the north. The place I thought I was going is imaginary, yet I have lived here most of my life.

PAINTING AND WRITING

I have a letter written by my great-great grandfather in 1902, full of the moment: "There are several cases of smallpox reported in Frederick." Yet despite the distance, the changes, there is an immediacy in the language. "Sim (a son-in-law) has sold $600 worth of wheat. He's thinking of buying a new buggy. I'm helping him paint his barn." It takes forever to paint one of those big barns. I think if I could find the place—somewhere southwest of Lyons—they'd still be at work, Sim on the high wooden ladder painting traditional barn red and the old man on the ground, painting the white trim around the doors and windows. So much work going into a structure that will fall down in fifty years, or less. It's awkward, difficult for any of us to know what to say. The past and the future are the same, finally. A time where you aren't. And you do what you do because it's the thing you do.

"Well, this has certainly been interesting."

"Yes."

"Yes, well this barn won't wait."

"No. You can't let your brush dry out."

"Yes, use it or lose it, as they say. Ha, ha."

"Say hello to everyone."

THUNDERSTORM WARNING

The National Weather Service has issued a severe thunder-storm warning effective until midnight. Expect heavy rain, hail, damaging winds, dizziness, nausea, headache, fainting, disorientation, uncertainty, loss of direction and the questioning of deeply held beliefs. Persons in the warning area should seek shelter immediately. If you are caught out in the open you should lie face down in a ditch or a depression.

BERRY PICKING

This time of year, mid-summer, we drive out the Matson road to pick thoughtberries, so called because once you spend a day picking you will think twice about ever doing it again. Thoughtberries don't grow in the deep woods but in the marginal, burned-over ground, in the scrub and scrap, in those awful swampy, bug-infested thickets. They are not plentiful. Sometimes it takes an hour of hard labor, picking the low stickery bushes to gather just a handful. Their scarcity must be the most of their appeal because, really, they aren't all that good. Small, tough and sour, they need a lot of sugar to make them palatable. There are not enough of them in these parts to make them a commercially viable product, but then in many parts of the country they don't grow at all.

THE BEAR'S MONEY

Every fall before he goes to sleep a bear will put away five or six hundred dollars. Money he got from garbage cans, mostly. People throw away thousands of dollars every day, and around here a lot of it goes to bears. But what good is money to a bear? I mean, how many places are there that a bear can spend it? It's a good idea to first locate the bear's den, in fall after the leaves are down. Back on one of the old logging roads you'll find a tall pine or spruce covered with scratch marks, the bear runes, which translate to something like "Keep out. That means you!" You can rest assured that the bear and his money are nearby, in a cave or in a space dug out under some big tree roots. When you return in winter, a long hike on snowshoes, the bear will be sound asleep. . . . In a month or two he'll wake, groggy, out of sorts, ready to bite something, ready to rip something to shreds . . . but by then you'll be long gone, back in town, spending like a drunken sailor.

HEY DIDDLE DIDDLE

I like the high times as much as anyone, the music and the jokes. I like the night, the wine, the shadows of trees on the path, the secret places on the periphery of the light, the breeze soughing in the tall pines. I can stay awake until ten o'clock, even eleven on weekends. Still, these days I'm happy when everything glides to a landing on the soft grass, when the guests have gone. I like the sound of the door closing, the latch catching, the light clicked off. But now it is nearly two in the morning and here I am lying awake. My dish is still out there somewhere, in the mad moonlight, last seen in the company of a spoon.

BLUE, BLUE DAY

Some days are so sad nothing will help, when love has gone, when the sunshine and clear sky only tease and mock you. Those days you feel like running away, going where no one knows your name. Like slinging the old Gibson over your shoulder and traveling the narrow road to the North where the gray sky fits your mood and the cold wind blows a different kind of trouble. Nothing up there but mosquito-infested swamp, 10,000 acres of hummocky muck, a thicket of alder and dogwood, a twisted tangle of complications where not even Hemingway would fish. But somebody, someday soon, somebody will come and put up a bed and breakfast and a gourmet coffee shop. There is only one true wilderness left to explore, those vast empty spaces in your head.

THREE DOGS

THE DOG OF THE DEAD

Sometimes I wake in the middle of the night and all is quiet except for a dog barking. A flat, repetitive barking that has the rhythmic qualities of someone driving a nail into a board. This is his job, the graveyard shift, to which he brings no enthusiasm but only a dogged persistence. He must be the dog of the dead since his owners never respond to his alarm.

IMAGINARY DOG

A man stands in the path holding a dog leash calling into woods, "Here Maggie. Here Maggie." When I approach he says, "Don't worry about my dog, she's awfully big but really gentle. She sometimes likes to jump up and lick people but she's never bitten anyone, well, there was the postman that time but he surprised her and it was really only a nip. . . Here Maggie. Here Maggie." I smile and pass by. There is no sign of a dog, only dense forest on either side of the path.

BLACK DOG

I don't own a dog and I don't want one, but every now and then a black dog accompanies me on my walk out on Winter Road, which is strange because there are no houses nearby, yet he seems well fed and content. He usually approaches from behind silently and walks alongside me. The first time he appeared it caused me to jump, but I've grown to expect him. As company he is only a little better than my own thoughts, ranging ahead or lagging behind to sniff at something in the ditch. We walk along, each without acknowledging the other, and when we part at the end of my hike neither of us says good-bye.

OLD MAN WINTER

Old man Winter doesn't like anything. He doesn't like dogs or cats or squirrels or birds, especially seagulls, or children or smart-ass college students. He doesn't like loggers or environmentalists or snowmobilers or skiers in their stupid lycra outfits. He doesn't like Christmas or television. He doesn't like bureaucrats, lawyers or politicians. There is a thing or two he could say to the host of the local talk-radio show but he knows for a fact that the son-of-a-bitch does the broadcast from his condo in Florida. He's pissed off about the OPEC oil conspiracy and the conspiracy of gas station owners to raise prices. He doesn't like foreigners and he doesn't like his neighbors (not that he has many); when they finally die they just leave their junk all over the yard. He doesn't like that. He doesn't like the look of the sky right now, either, overcast, a kind of jaundice color. He hates that. And that stand of spruce trees behind the house turning black in the dusk . . . . The way it gets dark earlier every day. He doesn't like that.

CONJURER

After years of practice you are able to produce the illusion of a human figure. A man, perhaps, wearing a dark suit, a middle-aged, more-or-less law-abiding, productive citizen. The finer points, however, still elude you. For one thing, you've gotten the ears way too large, the hair is unruly, unkempt looking and the sleeves of his jacket and the legs of his pants are too long, or else his arms and legs are too short. The brown shoes are on the wrong feet. No matter how you try the figure isn't quite right. On the other hand, fog and trees are fairly easy to conjure up and help to mask the errors. The droplets of water weighing down the delicate needles of the tall pines gives the scene a sort of oriental look, a kind of ancient dignity. And it gives the figure a rather contemplative aspect, the monk alone in the wilderness. But now the suit looks out of place. . . . Passersby will say, "Did you see that goofy looking guy over there in the trees?" "Goofy, yes . . . but very well-dressed." Sharper eyes will notice that the details are wrong but few will question that this is truly a human being.

JACKSTRAW

You look for deeper meanings in things. There are signs and portents, though sometimes you deny it. You find special significance in certain places and days, the cottage by the lake, Christmas, a certain Chinese restaurant in Winnipeg, your birthday, and set them up like signposts marking the passage of your life. One after another they multiply until you're surrounded by a forest of sticks. Jackstraws. Touch one and they all fall down. Jack Straw, head full of hay, reading long boring books, waiting for the mail, watching the days go by. Here it is Sunday morning and there's no one downtown but the loony and dysfunctional. There's Old One-Eye who recently returned from Jupiter, and the spooky Woman in White, Tom Drooley, Mr. Ozone Peepot, Euclid and The Motorcycle Queen, Mr. Occupant, Goofy Walker, Old Man Winter, still wearing his down parka. It's spring. It's April Fool's. It's the Easter parade! Grab your hat and let's get in line!

SOMERSAULT

Some children did handsprings or cartwheels. Those of us who were less athletically gifted did what we called somersaults, really a kind of forward roll. Head down in the summer grass, a push with the feet, then the world flipped upside-down and around. Your feet, which had been behind you, now stretched out in front. It was fun and we did it, laughing, again and again. Yet, as fun as it was, most of us, at some point, quit doing somersaults. But only recently, someone at Evening Rest (Managed Care for Seniors) discovered the potential value of somersaults as physical and emotional therapy for the aged, a recapturing of youth, perhaps. Every afternoon, weather permitting, the old people, despite their feeble protests, are led or wheeled onto the lawn, where each is personally and individually aided in the heels-over-head tumble into darkness. When the wind is right you can hear, even at this distance, the crying of those who have fallen and are unable to rise.

FLIGHT

Past mishaps might be attributed to an incomplete understanding of the laws of aerodynamics or perhaps even to a more basic failure of the imagination, but were to be expected. Remember, this is solo flight unencumbered by bicycle parts, aluminum and nylon or even feathers. A *tour de force*, really. There's a lot of running and flapping involved and as you get older and heavier, a lot more huffing and puffing. But on a bright day like today with a strong headwind blowing up from the sea, when, having slipped the surly bonds of common sense and knowing she is watching, waiting in breathless anticipation, you send yourself hurtling down the long, green slope to the cliffs, who knows? You might just make it.

THE NAME

Instead of an idea a name comes to you, a name that no longer has any connection to the owner of the name. It comes as sound merely, rhythmic, musical, exotic and foreign to your ears, a sound full of distance and mystery. A name such as Desmond Tutu, Patrice Lamumba or Menachem Begin. You forget the names of acquaintances and the name of your first true love but this name comes to you. It repeats like a tune in your head. It refuses to go away, becomes a kind of mental mumbling. You say it to yourself over and over. It is your mantra, "Boutros Boutros Ghali...." Then suddenly as it came, the name vanishes.

Deep in the night, long after your own name has flown away, a voice wakes you from a sound sleep, a voice clear and certain as the voice that summoned Elijah, saying "Oksana Baiul."

Louis Jenkins lives in Duluth, Minnesota. His poems have been published in numerous literary magazines and anthologies. Among his books of poetry are *An Almost Human Gesture* (Eighties Press and Ally Press, 1987), *All Tangled Up With the Living* (Nineties Press, 1991), *Nice Fish: New and Selected Prose Poems* (Holy Cow! Press, 1995), winner of the Minnesota Book Award, and *Just Above Water* (Holy Cow! Press, 1997). He has read his poems on *A Prairie Home Companion* and was a featured poet at the Geraldine R. Dodge Poetry Festival in 1996. Two of his prose poems were published in *The Best American Poetry* 1999 (Scribner).